Wild Life LOL!™
Bison

Get ready for some terri-BULL jokes!

SCHOLASTIC

Library of Congress Cataloging-in-Publication Data
Title: Bison
Description: New York, NY: Children's Press, an imprint of Scholastic Inc., 2020. | Series: Wild Life LOL! | Includes index.
Identifiers: LCCN 2019006053| ISBN 9780531240359 (library binding) | ISBN 9780531234884 (paperback)
Subjects: LCSH: Bison—Juvenile literature.
Classification: LCC QL737.U53 B547 2020 | DDC 599.64/3—dc23

Produced by Spooky Cheetah Press

Design by Anna Tunick Tabachnik

Contributing Jokester: J. E. Bright

Printed in Heshan, China 62

SCHOLASTIC, CHILDREN'S PRESS, WILD LIFE LOL!™, and associated logos are trademarks and/or registered trademarks of
Scholastic Inc.

1 2 3 4 5 6 7 8 9 10 R 29 28 27 26 25 24 23 22 21 20

Scholastic Inc., 557 Broadway, New York, NY 10012.

Photographs ©: cover, spine: Christina Krutz/Robert Harding Picture Library; cover speech bubbles and throughout: pijama61/
iStockphoto; cover speech bubbles and throughout: Astarina/Shutterstock; back cover and throughout: Isselee/Dreamstime;
3 top: dmbaker/iStockphoto; 3 bottom: abzerit/iStockphoto; 4: Tim Fitzharris/Minden Pictures; 5 left: Nowik Sylwia/Shutterstock;
5 right: Ashestosky/Dreamstime; 6-7: R9_RoNaLdO/iStockphoto; 8-9: jskiba/iStockphoto; 10-11: paulafrench/iStockphoto; 12 top:
SBTheGreenMan/iStockphoto; 12 bottom: Clément Philippe/age fotostock; 13 top: O.S. Fisher/Shutterstock; 13 bottom: erniedecker/
iStockphoto; 14: Jim Brandenburg/Minden Pictures; 15 left: Brad Sharp/age fotostock; 15 right: Uwe Walz/Getty Images; 16-17
background: Brzozowska/iStockphoto; 16 bottom left: wrangel/iStockphoto; 16 center: Ken Gillespie/Alamy Images; 17 left: sarkophoto/
iStockphoto; 17 right: JohnPitcher/iStockphoto; 18-19: R9_RoNaLdO/iStockphoto; 20: Linda Blair/Dreamstime; 21 left: Sumio Harada/
Minden Pictures; 21 right: Stefonlinton/iStockphoto; 22-23: brentawp/iStockphoto; 24-25: Daryl Mitchell/Flickr; 25 bottom right:
dmbaker/iStockphoto; 26 left: Robert Clifford Magis/National Geographic/Getty Images; 26 right: Corbis/Getty Images; 27 left: Laura
Grier/Getty Images; 27 right: EyeJoy/iStockphoto; 28 left: Mumemories/iStockphoto; 28 right: GlobalP/iStockphoto; 29 top: borchee/
iStockphoto; 29 bottom left: missanzi/Shutterstock; 30 map: Jim McMahon/Mapman®; 30 bottom: Steve Hinch Photography; 31: Steve
Hinch Photography; 32: codyphotography/Getty Images.

TABLE OF CONTENTS

COW-abunga!

MEET THE MASSIVE BISON

Are you ready to be amazed and amused? Keep reading. This book is massively entertaining!

LoL!
What's the difference between a car and a bison? **A car has only one horn.**

This is so a-MOO-sing!

At a Glance

Where do they live? → American bison are found only in the United States and Canada.

What do they do? → Bison spend much of their time eating.

What do they eat? → Bison are plant-eaters.

What do they look like? → Bison are huge animals with giant heads, horns, and shoulder humps.

How big are they? →

HINT: You're smaller. Check this out:

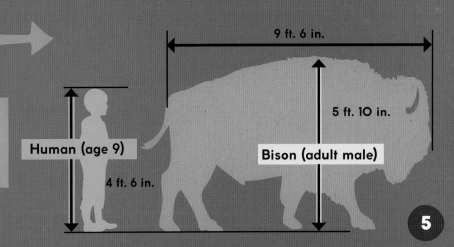

9 ft. 6 in.

5 ft. 10 in.

Human (age 9)

Bison (adult male)

4 ft. 6 in.

5

LIFE ON THE PRAIRIE

Bison make their home in open areas of grassland called prairies. They are also raised on ranches.

Let's Hang Out!
Bison are social animals. They live in big groups called herds.

LOL!
What did the comedian say to the bison?
Stop me if you've HERD this one before.

Bunches of Bison

A bison herd can contain between 20 and 1,000 animals, depending on the time of year.

Just Us Girls

Female bison are called cows. Cows and their young make up the biggest herds.

Male Bonding

Males are called bulls. Some bulls form smaller herds together. Others live in pairs or alone.

FAST FACT
Bison that live on ranches are often raised to be eaten.

A BISON'S BODY

Bison are the largest **mammals** in North America. They are built tough!

Standing Tall
Male bison can be as big and heavy as a car. Females are slightly smaller.

WACKY FACT:
Bison have poor eyesight, but their senses of hearing and smell are excellent.

mammals: animals that produce milk to feed their young

Over the Hump
Bison have humps on their backs. The humps are made of muscle.

Watch Out!
Two sharp horns are used for defense.

MOO-ve along, buddy!

Cool Beard!
Shaggy hair keeps the bison warm in cold weather.

WAIT! THESE ARE NOT BISON

These are buffaloes! People often call bison buffaloes, but they are two different animals. Here's how to tell them apart.

Beep, Beep!
Buffaloes have longer horns than bison.

Very Distant Relatives
Buffaloes live in Africa and Asia, not in North America.

Take It Down a Notch
A buffalo's head and neck are smaller than a bison's.

WACKY FACT:
Here's one similarity between bison and buffaloes. Both are great swimmers!

SEASONAL CHANGES

Bison live in places with freezing winters and hot summers. Here's how they change to survive.

Bison bodies are covered in fur. This extra layer keeps them comfortable, even in freezing temperatures.

Bison shed their shaggy coats. When temperatures rise, they rub on trees or on the ground to help loosen the hair.

winter

I'm never going to that barber again!

spring

fall

Little by little, the bison's thick coat starts growing again.

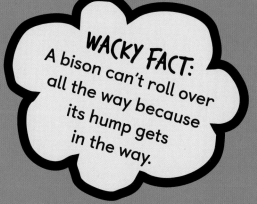

WACKY FACT: A bison can't roll over all the way because its hump gets in the way.

summer

Mosquitoes and flies bite the bison through their short summer coats. To stop the itching, bison roll back and forth in the dirt. This activity is called wallowing.

WATCH MY MOVES!

Bison don't let their huge bodies slow them down. Look at all the cool stuff they can do!

THAT'S EXTREME!
Bison can jump as high as 6 feet.

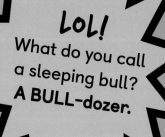

LOL!
What do you call a sleeping bull?
A BULL-dozer.

Fast Feet

Bison can run faster than the fastest adult! They can reach 35 miles per hour.

migration: moving throughout the year to find food and water

Super Swimmers

Bison move from place to place throughout the year to find food and water. This is called **migration**. If bison have to cross rivers . . . they just swim!

Dynamite Diggers

Bison can use their heads like bulldozers, plowing through snow to find buried food.

SHARING THE PRAIRIE

Bison are not alone on the prairie. They have a lot of neighbors. Some are helpful, but others . . . not so much!

I help bison by eating insects out of their fur. Yum!

magpie

Bison kick up the ground as they feed. I eat the grass and seeds that get stirred up.

prairie dog

CHEW ON THIS

Bison are so big, it's hard to believe they eat only plants. Of course, it takes a lot of grass to fill these animals up!

MOO-ving Right Along
Bison have to keep moving as they **graze** so they don't chew up all the grass in one area.

Time to Digest
A bison's stomach has four chambers. The animal chews its food four times before it is fully digested.

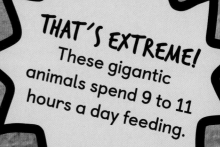

THAT'S EXTREME!
These gigantic animals spend 9 to 11 hours a day feeding.

Grassless Winter
In winter there is hardly any grass. Bison eat other plants, called lichens and moss.

You haven't lived until you've licked lichen!

graze: to feed on grass that is growing in a field

STARTING A FAMILY

In summer, male and female herds come together to **mate**. This big gathering is called a rut. Here's how it works.

Are we there yet? Don't want to be late to mate!

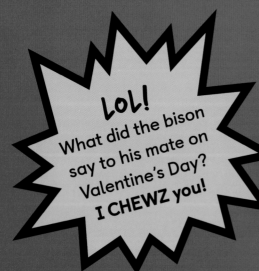

1

LOL!
What did the bison say to his mate on Valentine's Day?
I CHEWZ you!

A Long Trip

Some bison may travel as far as 150 miles to reach the meeting point for the rut.

mate: to join together to have babies

WACKY FACT: Bison use loud grunts and snorts to communicate.

Take THAT!

Let's go to the CALF-eteria!

2

3

The Competition

Male bison compete over females. They butt heads and use their horns to wrestle. The winner gets to mate with the female.

Here Comes Baby!

The following summer, baby bison, called calves, are born.

AS BABY GROWS

Female bison have just one baby a year. Look at how quickly they grow up!

LOL!
What did the mama bison say to her son as he ran across the field? "Bi-son!"

1

A Big Baby!

A newborn bison weighs about 50 pounds. It has reddish fur and drinks its mother's milk.

2

Snack Time

After two weeks, the calf also starts eating grass. It stays close to its mom at all times.

3

Growing Fast

In two months, the calf starts growing its hump and horns. Soon after that it begins to turn dark brown.

ANCIENT BISON

Scientists think the first bison came to North America more than 200,000 years ago. They know about these bison ancestors from **fossils** like this one.

What's Your Name?
This is *Bison latifrons*. It's also known as the longhorn or giant bison.

WACKY FACT: Latifrons means "wide forehead"!

Massive Body
Giant bison were about 8 feet tall. That's bigger than the tallest NBA player!

fossils: plants or animals from millions of years ago preserved as rock

BISON AND PEOPLE

Bison have a long—and complicated—history with people.

Hunters shot bison from inside—and on top of—moving trains.

Pre-1700s

For thousands of years, Native American tribes, or nations, hunted bison for fur and meat. They killed only as many animals as they needed to live.

1800s

In the early 1800s, about 60 million bison lived in North America. Then settlers moved across the land and started hunting them in huge numbers.

Honk again, and I'll show you real horns!

1894

By this time, fewer than 1,000 bison were left in the United States. In 1894, the U.S. government passed a law against hunting bison.

Today

Today there are almost 30,000 wild bison. Yellowstone National Park is home to the largest wild herd on Earth. Other bison live on ranches.

27

Bison Cousins

These are bison's closest cousins.

LOL! How did the yak win the lottery? It hit the YAK-pot!

yaks

water buffaloes

We live in wet grasslands, swamps, and river valleys in Asia.

Please note: Animals are not shown to scale.

cows

We live on ranches and farms around the world.

It's easy to see we're related!

We carry heavy loads in the mountains of Asia.

European bison

Bet you can guess where we live!

The Wild Life

Look at this map of the world. The areas in red show where American bison live today. We want our bison to continue having **habitats** to live in. Otherwise, one day there might not be any red left on this map.

Canada

United States

Home, home on the range . . .

habitats: the places where a plant or an animal makes its home

Bringing the Bison Back

In 1905, there were fewer than 1,000 bison in North America. That year, the New York Zoological Society (NYZS) founded the American Bison Society.

Keepers at NYZS's Bronx Zoo cared for and protected the bison and then transported them to their natural ranges in the western United States. These animals helped repopulate the small herds living in the wild.

What Can You Do?

Talk to an adult about supporting the American Bison Society or the Bronx Zoo directly.

You can also virtually adopt a bison through organizations such as the National Wildlife Federation (NWF) and the World Wildlife Fund (WWF).

INDEX

ABOUT THIS BOOK

This book is a laugh-out-loud early-grade adaptation of *Bison* by Mara Grunbaum. *Bison* was originally published by Scholastic as part of its Nature's Children series in 2019.

Have you HERD enough?